A+ books

DINOSAUR FACT DIG

VELOCIRAPTOR
AND OTHER RAPTORS
THE NEED-TO-KNOW FACTS

BY

REBECCA RISSMAN

Consultant: Mathew J. Wedel, PhD
Associate Professor
Western University of Health Services

raintree
a Capstone company — publishers for children

Raintree is an imprint of Capstone Global Library Limited, a company incorporated in England and Wales having its registered office at 264 Banbury Road, Oxford, OX2 7DY – Registered company number: 6695582

www.raintree.co.uk
myorders@raintree.co.uk

Edited by Michelle Hasselius
Designed by Kazuko Collins
Picture research by Wanda Winch
Production by Gene Bentdahl

ISBN 978 1 474 71942 1
20 19 18 17 16
10 9 8 7 6 5 4 3 2 1

British Library Cataloguing in Publication Data
A full catalogue record for this book is available from the British Library.

ACKNOWLEDGEMENTS
All images by Jon Hughes except: MapArt (maps), Shutterstock: Elena Elisseeva, green gingko leaf, Jiang Hongyan, yellow gingko leaf, Taigi, paper background

Every effort has been made to contact copyrightholders of material reproduced in this book. Any omissions will be rectified in subsequent printings if notice is given to the publisher.

All the internet addresses (URLs) given in this book were valid at the time of going to press. However, due to the dynamic nature of the internet, some addresses may have changed, or sites may have changed or ceased to exist since publication. While the author and publisher regret any inconvenience this may cause readers, no responsibility for any such changes can be accepted by either the author or the publisher.

Printed in China.

CONTENTS

Raptors were a fast, smart and deadly group of dinosaurs. They slashed at prey with fierce teeth and razor sharp claws.

Raptors lived between 125 and 65 million years ago. Thanks to the film *Jurassic Park*, Velociraptor is one of the most well known raptors. But there were many other fierce raptors that roamed the Earth. Learn about Microraptor, Buitreraptor, Bambiraptor and other dinosaurs in the raptor group.

AVIMIMUS

PRONOUNCED: AH-vee-MY-mus

NAME MEANING: bird mimic

TIME PERIOD LIVED: Late Cretaceous Period, about 80 to 70 million years ago

LENGTH: 1.1 metres (3.5 feet)

WEIGHT: 11 kilograms (25 pounds)

TYPE OF EATER: omnivore

PHYSICAL FEATURES: feathers, long legs, short arms and a beak

AVIMIMUS had claws on its hands and feet. It used them when hunting small animals. The dinosaur also ate plants.

Avimimus lived in the deserts of China and Mongolia.

N
W E
S

where this dinosaur lived

AVIMIMUS looked like a bird. It was covered with feathers but couldn't fly.

AVIMIMUS could run very quickly. Its short, strong tail helped it balance while running.

BAMBIRAPTOR

PRONOUNCED: BAM-bee-RAP-tur

NAME MEANING: named after the character in the Disney film *Bambi* because of its small size

TIME PERIOD LIVED: Late Cretaceous Period, about 75 million years ago

LENGTH: 0.8 metres (30 inches)

WEIGHT: 2 kilograms (4.5 pounds)

TYPE OF EATER: carnivore

PHYSICAL FEATURES: travelled on two legs, had feathers

BAMBIRAPTOR could move its arms the way birds move their wings. But it could not fly.

BAMBIRAPTOR was a small, smart predator.

Some scientists believe **BAMBIRAPTOR** fossils are actually from a baby Saurornitholestes.

BAMBIRAPTOR fossils were first discovered in 1995.

Bambiraptor lived in what is now Montana, USA.

BAMBIRAPTOR may have been able to climb trees.

N
W E
S

where this dinosaur lived

BEIPIAOSAURUS

PRONOUNCED: bay-pyow-SAWR-us

NAME MEANING: Beipiao lizard, because fossils were discovered near Beipiao, China

TIME PERIOD LIVED: Early Cretaceous Period, about 127 to 121 million years ago

LENGTH: 1.8 metres (6 feet)

WEIGHT: 41 kilograms (90 pounds)

TYPE OF EATER: herbivore

PHYSICAL FEATURES: feathers, short legs, strong arms and a beak

BEIPIAOSAURUS used its long claws to pull down leaves from trees and protect itself from predators.

BEIPIAOSAURUS used its strong beak to eat leaves and fruit.

BEIPIAOSAURUS was covered in long, brightly coloured feathers. The dinosaur may have used its feathers to communicate with other dinosaurs.

Beipiaosaurus lived in the forests of what is now China.

where this dinosaur lived

N
W   E
S

BUITRERAPTOR

PRONOUNCED: BWEE-tree-RAP-tur

NAME MEANING: vulture thief

TIME PERIOD LIVED: Cretaceous Period, about 90 million years ago

LENGTH: 0.6 to 1.5 metres (2 to 5 feet)

WEIGHT: 3 kilograms (6.6 pounds)

TYPE OF EATER: carnivore

PHYSICAL FEATURES: small body, feathers and two short wings

It took scientists 10 days to dig the first **BUITRERAPTOR** fossil out of stone.

Buitreraptor lived in the deserts and forests of what is now Argentina.

N
W E
S

where this dinosaur lived

BUITRERAPTOR had wings, but it could not fly. It probably couldn't jump or climb very well.

BUITRERAPTOR was about the size of a cockerel.

BUITRERAPTOR had a strange head shape. Paleontologists think it helped the dinosaur catch fish and other small prey.

CAUDIPTERYX

PRONOUNCED: KAW-dip-TER-ix

NAME MEANING: tail feathers

TIME PERIOD LIVED: Early Cretaceous Period, about 125 to 122 million years ago

LENGTH: 0.9 metres (3 feet)

WEIGHT: 7 kilograms (15 pounds)

TYPE OF EATER: omnivore

PHYSICAL FEATURES: long feathers on arms and tail, strong legs, short arms and beak

CAUDIPTERYX swallowed rocks. The dinosaur used the rocks in its stomach to help break down food.

CAUDIPTERYX had short, feathered arms, but it could not fly. It ran and jumped.

Caudipteryx lived in the wetlands and forests of what is now China.

N
W — E
S

where this dinosaur lived

CAUDIPTERYX had small, sharp teeth inside its beak. It ate plants and small animals.

DEINONYCHUS

PRONOUNCED: dye-NON-i-kus

NAME MEANING: terrible claw

TIME PERIOD LIVED: Cretaceous Period, about 118 to 110 million years ago

LENGTH: 3 metres (10 feet)

WEIGHT: 50 kilograms (110 pounds)

TYPE OF EATER: carnivore

PHYSICAL FEATURES: travelled on two legs, as tall as an adult human

Deinonychus lived in what is now the United States.

☐ where this dinosaur lived

N
W E
S

DEINONYCHUS probably hunted in packs.

DEINONYCHUS had a large brain and eyes. Paleontologists think the dinosaur was smart.

The Velociraptor featured in the 1993 film *Jurassic Park* was actually modelled after DEINONYCHUS.

FALCARIUS

PRONOUNCED: FAL-car-EE-us

NAME MEANING: sickle cutter

TIME PERIOD LIVED: Early Cretaceous Period, about 125 million years ago

LENGTH: 4 metres (13 feet)

WEIGHT: 100 kilograms (220 pounds)

TYPE OF EATER: herbivore

PHYSICAL FEATURES: long body, feathers and long, curved claws

Falcarius lived in the prairies and forests of what is now the United States.

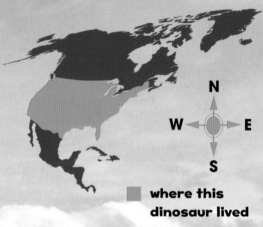

where this dinosaur lived

FALCARIUS may have used its feathers to stay warm.

FALCARIUS' curved claws were up to 13 centimetres (5 inches) long.

FALCARIUS had leaf-shaped teeth. Paleontologists think it ate plants.

More than 3,000 FALCARIUS bones were found at a giant dinosaur dig in Utah, USA.

FALCARIUS was one of the first meat-eating dinosaurs to become a herbivore. The dinosaur ate meat at first, then began eating only plants.

MICRORAPTOR

PRONOUNCED: MIKE-row-RAP-tur

NAME MEANING: tiny thief

TIME PERIOD LIVED: Early Cretaceous Period, about 125 to 122 million years ago

LENGTH: 0.8 metres (2.5 feet)

WEIGHT: 0.6 kilogram (1.3 pounds)

TYPE OF EATER: carnivore

PHYSICAL FEATURES: travelled on two legs, covered in feathers

Like today's pelicans, **MICRORAPTOR** swallowed fish whole.

MICRORAPTOR was a small dinosaur with long feathers. Some scientists think the dinosaur looked like a giant butterfly from a distance.

MICRORAPTOR could not fly, but it may have glided from tree to tree.

Microraptor lived in the forests of what is now China.

where this dinosaur lived

PROTARCHAEOPTERYX

PRONOUNCED: PROH-tar-kee-OP-ter-iks

NAME MEANING: first ancient wing

TIME PERIOD LIVED: Early Cretaceous Period, about 135 million years ago

LENGTH: 0.9 metres (3 feet)

WEIGHT: 2 kilograms (5 pounds)

TYPE OF EATER: omnivore

PHYSICAL FEATURES: feathers, short arms and strong legs

The dinosaur's body was about the size of a turkey.

PROTARCHAEOPTERYX could not fly. Instead it ran on its strong back legs.

At first paleontologists thought **PROTARCHAEOPTERYX** was a bird. They later discovered it was related to small feathered dinosaurs, such as Incisivosaurus.

Protarchaeopteryx lived in the wetlands and forests of what is now China.

N
W E
S

where this dinosaur lived

SAURORNITHOLESTES

PRONOUNCED: sore-OR-nith-oh-LESS-tease

NAME MEANING: lizard-bird thief

TIME PERIOD LIVED: Late Cretaceous Period, about 75 million years ago

LENGTH: 1.8 metres (6 feet)

WEIGHT: 14 kilograms (30 pounds)

TYPE OF EATER: carnivore

PHYSICAL FEATURES: sharp teeth and claws, travelled on two legs

SAURORNITHOLESTES was about as long as a small dog, such as a terrier.

SAURORNITHOLESTES ate small prey, such as lizards and birds. It may have also been a scavenger.

Saurornitholestes lived in what are now the United States and Canada.

N
W E
S

where this dinosaur lived

Like many raptors, **SAURORNITHOLESTES** had a sharp claw on each back leg.

TROODON

PRONOUNCED: TROH-o-don

NAME MEANING: wounding tooth

TIME PERIOD LIVED: Late Cretaceous Period, about 74 to 65 million years ago

LENGTH: 1.8 metres (6 feet)

WEIGHT: 50 kilograms (110 pounds)

TYPE OF EATER: carnivore

PHYSICAL FEATURES: travelled on two legs, sharp teeth and claws

TROODON had a large brain. Scientists believe it may have been one of the smartest dinosaurs.

A female **TROODON** laid two eggs at a time. She would sit on the eggs to keep them warm until they hatched.

TROODON had long, curved and jagged teeth. They helped the dinosaur eat small animals, such as lizards and insects.

Troodon lived in what are now the United States and Canada.

N
W E
S

where this dinosaur lived

VARIRAPTOR

PRONOUNCED: VA-ree-RAP-tur

NAME MEANING: thief from Var River

TIME PERIOD LIVED: Late Cretaceous Period, about 70 million years ago

LENGTH: 1.8 metres (6 feet)

WEIGHT: 45 kilograms (100 pounds)

TYPE OF EATER: carnivore

PHYSICAL FEATURES: travelled on two legs, claws on hands and feet, sharp teeth

Like many raptors **VARIRAPTOR** ran quickly on two legs.

VARIRAPTOR'S arm bones show that it could slash its prey with a lot of force.

VARIRAPTOR was a small, smart predator. It spent much of its time hunting prey.

Very few **VARIRAPTOR** fossils have been found.

Variraptor lived in what is now France.

N
W E
S

■ where this dinosaur lived

VELOCIRAPTOR

PRONOUNCED: veh-LOSS-eh-RAP-tur

NAME MEANING: speedy thief

TIME PERIOD LIVED: Late Cretaceous Period, about 75 million years ago

LENGTH: 1.8 metres (6 feet)

WEIGHT: 15 kilograms (33 pounds)

TYPE OF EATER: carnivore

PHYSICAL FEATURES: feathers, sharp teeth, travelled on two legs

Velociraptor lived in Asia, in what are now Mongolia and China.

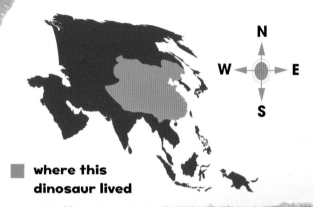

where this dinosaur lived

VELOCIRAPTOR hunted in packs.

VELOCIRAPTOR had a curved claw on each back foot. The claw was 7.6 centimetres (3 inches) long.

VELOCIRAPTOR killed prey with its long, sharp claws. The dinosaur also ate dinosaur eggs. It broke the eggs open with its sharp teeth.

GLOSSARY

BEAK hard, pointed part of an animal's mouth

CARNIVORE animal that eats only meat

COMMUNICATE share information, thoughts or feelings

CRETACEOUS PERIOD third period of the Mesozoic Era; the Cretaceous Period was from 145 to 65 million years ago

FOSSIL remains of an animal or plant from millions of years ago that have turned to rock

GLIDE move smoothly through the air; animals that glide do not flap their wings

HATCH come out of an egg

HERBIVORE animal that eats only plants

OMNIVORE animal that eats both plants and animals

PACK small group of animals that hunts together

PALEONTOLOGIST scientist who studies fossils

PRAIRIE large area of flat grassland

PREDATOR animal that hunts other animals for food

PREY animal hunted by another animal for food

PRONOUNCE say a word in a certain way

SCAVENGER animal that eats animals that are already dead

WETLAND area of land covered by water and plants; marshes, swamps and bogs are wetlands

COMPREHENSION QUESTIONS

1. What was Bambiraptor named after? Use the text to help you with your answer.

2. Raptors like Caudipteryx and Protarchaeopteryx were omnivores. What does "omnivore" mean?

3. Many raptors had feathers but could not fly. Name an animal today that has feathers but can't fly.

READ MORE

Dinosaurs (First Facts), Charlie Gardner (DK Publishing, 2012)

Velociraptor (All About Dinosaurs), Daniel Nunn (Raintree, 2015)

Velociraptor and other Raptors and Small Carnivores (Dinosaurs!), David West (Franklin Watts, 2013)

WEBSITES

www.nhm.ac.uk/discover/dino-directory/index.html

At this Natural History Museum website you can learn more about dinosaurs through sorting them by name, country and even body shape!

www.show.me.uk/section/dinosaurs

This website has loads of fun things to do and see, including a dinosaur mask you can download and print, videos, games, and Top Ten lists.

INDEX